Get ready  islands of Polynesia, a place full of amazing animals!

Have you ever met a gecko that can climb walls, a turtle that swims across oceans, or a fish with a funny name like Humuhumunukunukuapua'a?

What about a dolphin that loves to spin or a crab that can climb trees?

So, grab your imagination and get ready to dive into the tropical world of Polynesia, where nature is full of surprises!

CONTENTS

4 Polynesia
8 Hawaii
12 Samoa
13 American Samoa
14 Culture of the Samoan Islands
16 Green Sea Turtle
20 Kauila The Brave Sea Turtle
22 Hawaiian Monk Seal
26 Coconut Crab
28 Jackson's Chameleon
32 Feral Pigs
36 Kamapua'a, the Pig God of the Forest
38 Flying Fox
42 Geckos
46 The Guardian Mo'o Protectors of Water
48 Humpback Whale
52 The Legend of the Singing Whale
54 Spinner Dolphin

58 Giant Clam
60 Whale Shark
64 The Shark God Who Saved Sailors
66 Great Hammerhead Shark
70 Giant Pacific Octopus
74 The Octopus Who Held the World Together
76 Manta Ray
80 The Manta Ray's Moonlight Dance
82 Moray Eels
86 Sina and the Coconut Tree
88 Clownfish
92 Humuhumunukunukuapua'a Reef Triggerfish
94 Jellyfish
98 Roosters and Hens
102 Samoan White-Eye
106 'I'iwi Hawaiian Honeycreeper
108 'Ōhi'a Lehua
110 Nēnē Hawaiian Goose

Polynesia

Polynesia forms a huge triangle on the map, with Hawaii, New Zealand, and Easter Island at its corners.

Some islands in Polynesia are thousands of miles away from each other.

POLYNESIAN TRIANGLE

HAWAII

SAMOA

AMERICAN SAMOA

NEW ZEALAND

EASTER ISLAND

Pacific Ocean

Polynesia has more than 1,000 islands scattered across the Pacific Ocean.

The Pacific Ocean, which surrounds Polynesia, is the biggest and deepest ocean in the world.

4

Many islands, like Samoa and Hawaii, were made by volcanoes erupting underwater.

Coconut palms grow naturally on many islands, often near beaches.

Volcanic islands often have beaches with black sand instead of white.

Polynesia has two main seasons: the rainy season and the dry season.

Cool winds called "trade winds" blow gently across the islands to keep things comfortable.

Polynesia is famous for its giant waves, perfect for surfing.

The reefs around Polynesia are filled with colorful coral, fish, and sea creatures.

Some islands are atolls, ring-shaped islands made of coral that surround lagoons.

Low islands are flat, like atolls, while high islands, like Bora Bora, have mountains.

Many islands have waterfalls hidden in the jungle that you can only reach by hiking.

Hawaii

50th State

Hawaii is the only U.S. state made entirely of islands!

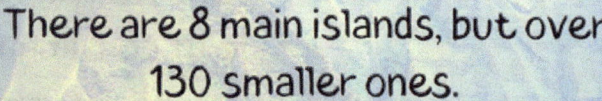

There are 8 main islands, but over 130 smaller ones.

Hawai'i (The Big Island)
The largest island, famous for its volcanoes, including Mauna Kea and Kilauea.

Maui (The Valley Isle)
Known for stunning beaches, the Road to Hana, and Haleakalā National Park.

O'ahu (The Gathering Place)
Home to Honolulu, Waikīkī Beach, and Pearl Harbor.

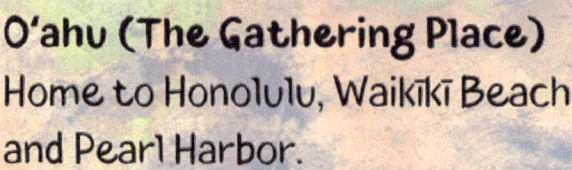

Kaua'i (The Garden Isle)
Famous for its lush rainforests, Waimea Canyon, and Nā Pali Coast.

Moloka'i (The Friendly Isle)
Known for its unspoiled beauty and rich Hawaiian traditions.

Lāna'i (The Pineapple Isle)
Once covered in pineapple plantations, now a quiet retreat.

Ni'ihau (The Forbidden Isle)
Privately owned, access is limited to residents and invited guests.

Kaho'olawe (The Target Isle)
Uninhabited and used for conservation efforts after being a military training site.

"Aloha" means hello, goodbye, and love. It's also about being kind and welcoming.

Hula Dance
Hula tells stories about Hawaiian history and nature.

Giving a flower lei is a way to show love and friendship.

Surfing started in Hawaii!

Hawaiians believe Pele, the goddess of fire, lives in the volcanoes.

Hawaii is famous for its pineapples and coconuts.

Mauna Kea in Hawaii is the tallest volcano in the world when measured from the ocean floor!

Samoa

Samoa has two main islands, Upolu and Savai'i.

Life moves slower in Samoa. People enjoy a relaxed and happy pace of life!

Like Hawaii, Samoa was formed by volcanoes.

The To Sua Ocean Trench is a famous natural swimming hole.

Samoa has waterfalls hidden in the jungle.

American Samoa

American Samoa is made up of 5 main islands and 2 tiny atolls in the Pacific Ocean.

The largest island is Tutuila, and it's where most people live.

American Samoa has some of the tallest sea cliffs in the world, rising high above the ocean!

The islands have special plants, like the Pometia pinnata (tava tree), that grow nowhere else.

Culture of the Samoan Islands

Fa'a Samoa means "The Samoan Way," a set of traditions about family and respect.

Men and women in Samoa wear traditional tattoos called tatau.

Traditional homes, called fale, have no walls and are open to the breeze.

Drumming is a big part of Samoan music and celebrations.

People weave mats from palm leaves for sleeping and ceremonies.

Samoan dancers twirl knives set on fire!

Samoans eat fresh fish, taro, and coconut dishes.

15

Green Sea Turtle

Green sea turtles spend most of their lives in the ocean, gliding through the water with their powerful flippers!

Adult green sea turtles mostly eat seagrass and algae, making them some of the only vegetarian sea turtles.

Even though they're called "green" sea turtles, their shells are usually brown or olive-colored. Their name comes from the greenish color of their body fat!

Green sea turtles have good eyesight and a strong sense of smell to help them find food.

They use their strong front flippers to swim, reaching speeds of up to 15 miles per hour!

Green sea turtles lay their eggs in sandy nests on beaches, usually at night.

Baby turtles, called hatchlings, are only about 2 inches (5 cm) long when they're born!

Hatchlings make a dash for the ocean right after hatching to escape predators on the beach.

These turtles travel long distances, sometimes over 1,000 miles, to return to the beach where they were born to lay eggs.

Adult green sea turtles can grow to be as big as a kitchen table and weigh as much as 700 pounds (317 kg)!

Unlike some animals, green sea turtles don't make noises. They're quiet as they swim and rest.

Kauila
The Brave Sea Turtle

Deep in the crystal-clear waters of Hawaii lived Kauila, a sea turtle with eyes as warm as sunlight.

Kauila was no ordinary turtle—she had magical powers and could take the shape of a young girl. Kauila loved the children of the island and often swam close to shore to watch them play.

One day, while playing on the beach, Kauila noticed some children had wandered too far into the water. A strong current was pulling them out to sea!

Kauila acted swiftly. She dove beneath the waves, her shell glowing like a golden lantern, and lifted the children onto her broad back. With mighty strokes, she carried them to the safety of the shore.

The villagers were amazed by Kauila's bravery. They built a stone shrine by the beach to honor her, and every evening, they told stories of the kind sea turtle who watched over the island's children.

Some say that when you see a sea turtle swimming near the shore, Kauila's spirit is still protecting the young.

Hawaiian Monk Seal

Hawaiian monk seals are one of only two seal species that live in warm tropical waters, and they are found only in Hawaii!

In Hawaiian, they're called 'Ilio holo i ka uaua, which means "dog that runs in rough water."

Hawaiian monk seals are excellent swimmers and can stay underwater for up to 20 minutes!

When they're tired, monk seals love to rest on sandy beaches. You might spot them snoozing in the sun!

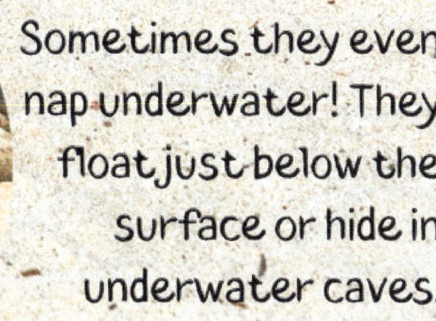

Sometimes they even nap underwater! They float just below the surface or hide in underwater caves.

These seals can weigh as much as 600 pounds (270 kg)—about the size of three refrigerators!

They have sensitive whiskers that help them feel movement in the water and find fish hiding in the sand.

They hunt alone rather than in groups, so they are called "monk" seals.

Some beaches in Hawaii have special zones where monk seals can rest safely, away from people.

Baby monk seals are called "pups." Pups have black fur when they're born and stay with their mothers for six weeks.

Coconut Crab

They are called coconut crabs because they can crack open coconuts with their strong claws to eat the yummy coconut inside.

Coconut crabs are the largest land-living crabs in the world! They can grow as big as a soccer ball!

These crabs can be blue, purple, or reddish-brown, which helps them blend in with their surroundings.

Coconut crabs are great climbers! They can climb tall coconut trees to get coconuts.

Coconut crabs live on tropical islands in the Indian and Pacific Oceans, including places like Polynesia.

Jackson's Chameleon

Their eyes can move separately, meaning they can look in two different directions at the same time!

Male Jackson's chameleons have three horns on their heads, like a tiny triceratops dinosaur!

Only the males have three horns. Female Jackson's chameleons don't have horns!

Jackson's chameleons can change colors! They change shades to blend in, show their mood, or communicate with other chameleons.

They have a super-long, sticky tongue that shoots out to catch insects from far away—almost like a built-in slingshot!

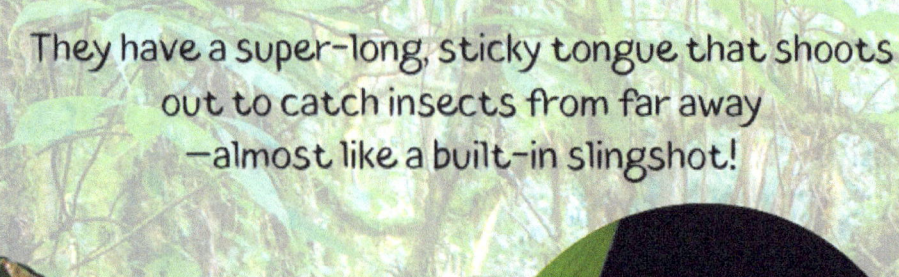

Unlike many reptiles that lay eggs, Jackson's chameleons give birth to live baby chameleons.

Jackson's chameleons live in trees and have special, strong feet and a tail that help them hold onto branches.

Jackson's chameleons love humid, rainy places. They drink water droplets from leaves after a rainstorm.

These chameleons move very slowly and carefully to avoid being spotted by predators and to sneak up on their prey.

Feral Pigs

Pigs were brought to Polynesia by early Polynesians as a food source, but some escaped and became wild.

Feral pigs live in groups called "sounders" that are made up of moms and babies. Adult males like to wander on their own.

Baby pigs, called piglets, are born in litters of up to 12 and have stripes on their backs when they're very young.

Cute

Feral pigs communicate with each other through squeals, grunts, and snorts.

Feral pigs love rolling around in mud to stay cool and protect their skin from bugs.

MUD SPA

They dig up soil with their snouts to find food, which can create holes in the ground.

Pigs have an amazing sense of smell and can sniff out food buried underground.

Their skin is thick and tough, which protects them from thorns and bushes as they move through the forest.

Their strong legs help them run fast and travel long distances to look for food.

They have rough, bristly fur that can be black, brown, or a mix of colors.

Kamapua'a, the Pig God of the Forest

In the misty forests of Hawaii, where ferns grew as tall as houses, lived Kamapua'a, the pig spirit. With tusks sharp as crescent moons and a laugh that echoed through the hills, Kamapua'a was a magical creature who could bring life to the land.

One day, Kamapua'a saw a barren plain scorched by the sun. "This land is thirsty," he grunted, pawing the dry earth with his powerful hooves. He dug deep into the ground, and water gushed forth like a fountain, creating streams that danced through the land. Soon, plants began to sprout—first tiny blades of grass, then mighty trees bursting with fruit.

But Pele, the fiery volcano goddess, noticed Kamapuaʻa's work and grew jealous. "This is my land!" she roared, sending rivers of lava to cover the forest. Kamapuaʻa, quick as a flash, turned into a boar and raced ahead of the molten fire.

Wherever Kamapuaʻa's hooves touched, the land remained green, and his laughter echoed as he vanished into the forest.

To this day, Hawaiians say Kamapuaʻa's spirit lives in the trees, and when the wind whistles through the leaves, it's his playful laugh.

Flying Fox

They have big, pointed ears that help them hear well, even in the dark.

Their wings are long and leathery, helping them glide through the air for long distances.

These bats are called "fruit bats" because they mostly eat juicy fruits like mangoes, bananas, and papayas.

They sleep upside down, hanging by their feet from tree branches.

They have strong thumbs with sharp claws that help them grab branches and hold on tight.

Flying foxes are the largest bats in the world, with wings that can stretch as wide as a kid's bed!

Flying foxes live in large groups called colonies or camps, usually in tall trees.

Flying foxes have a great sense of smell that helps them find ripe fruit and flowers.

Their noses look like tiny fox faces, which is why they're called "flying foxes"!

These bats have soft, fluffy fur around their neck and body, which helps keep them warm.

Flying foxes are social and like to chat with each other using squeaks and clicks.

Baby flying foxes, called pups, cling to their mom's belly for the first few weeks of life.

Geckos

Common house geckos are small lizards that love climbing walls, windows, and even ceilings!

They have special sticky pads on their toes, which help them climb smooth surfaces —even upside down!

They don't have eyelids, so they can't blink. Instead, they lick their eyes to keep them clean and moist.

Their tail can be as long as their whole body, helping them balance and steer when they climb.

If a predator grabs a gecko by its tail, the tail can break off! The gecko then grows a new one over time.

Geckos have excellent night vision, which helps them see in the dark when they're hunting.

House geckos are nocturnal, which means they come out mostly at night to look for food.

These geckos can change their color slightly to blend in with their surroundings, which helps them hide from predators.

Geckos love to eat bugs like mosquitoes, flies, and moths. They're like little pest controllers!

If you hear little chirping sounds at night, it might be a house gecko calling to its friends!

These geckos are harmless to people. They are more scared of us than we are of them!

The Guardian Mo'o Protectors of Water

In the heart of a lush Hawaiian valley, there lay a secret pond that sparkled like green emeralds under the sun. This was no ordinary pond, for it was watched over by Kihawahine, a mo'o—a mystical dragon-lizard spirit with shimmering scales that glistened like gold in the moonlight.

The villagers whispered tales of Kihawahine's magic. "She blesses the water with life," they would say. Her pond teemed with glittering fish, and the water was so pure it sparkled like starlight. But Kihawahine had one rule: the people must care for the land and never harm the water.

One year, the rains disappeared, and the stream that fed the pond fell silent. The water turned still, and the fish swam no more. A little girl named Lehua, who loved the pond dearly, dreamed of Kihawahine one night. "Clear the stones blocking the stream," the moʻo whispered, her voice soft as ripples.

Lehua gathered the villagers, and together they worked to move the stones. Water flowed down the mountain once again, filling the pond. The villagers cheered and thanked Kihawahine. From then on, they cared for the pond and the land around it, knowing Kihawahine was always watching.

Humpback Whale

Humpbacks can hold their breath for up to 30 minutes underwater before coming up for air.

Humpbacks have long flippers—up to 16 feet (4.8 m)! Their flippers help them turn and steer in the water.

Male humpbacks sing loud, beautiful songs that can last up to 20 minutes and be heard miles away!

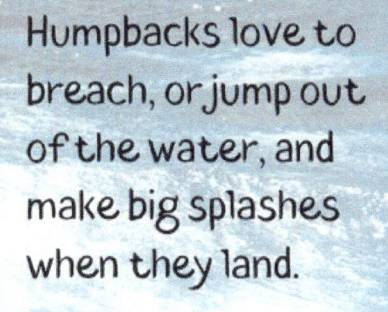

Humpbacks love to breach, or jump out of the water, and make big splashes when they land.

Humpbacks are amazing travelers! They migrate thousands of miles from warm tropical waters to colder feeding grounds.

Humpback whales are HUGE! They can grow as long as a school bus and weigh as much as 10 elephants.

49

Baby humpback whales are called calves. They are about 12-15 feet (3,5 – 4,5 M) long when they're born!

Calves stay close to their mothers for about a year, learning to swim and eat.

Humpbacks migrate to warmer waters to give birth, where the water is nice and cozy for their calves.

Humpbacks don't have teeth! Instead, they use baleen plates in their mouths to filter out food from the water.

They work together to blow bubbles in a circle to trap fish, which is called "bubble-net feeding."

Each humpback has a unique pattern on its tail, like a fingerprint. Scientists use this to tell them apart.

Their big tails are called "flukes," and they use them to propel themselves through the water.

The Legend of the Singing Whale

Long ago, in the vast blue ocean around the Polynesian islands, there lived a giant whale named Tangaloa, the guardian of the deep. His voice was so powerful that his songs could calm storms and guide lost sailors home.

One day, a young boy named Tui was fishing with his father when a fierce storm swept across the sea. Their canoe rocked wildly, and Tui called out, "Please, someone help us!"

From the depths came a low, rumbling song. Tangaloa, the great whale, rose from the water, his enormous body shining like the moon.
"Do not be afraid," Tangaloa sang.
With his gentle voice, he calmed the wind and waves, creating a safe path back to the island.

To this day, Polynesians believe that whales sing to keep the ocean safe and remind people of their connection to the sea and their ancestors.

Spinner Dolphin

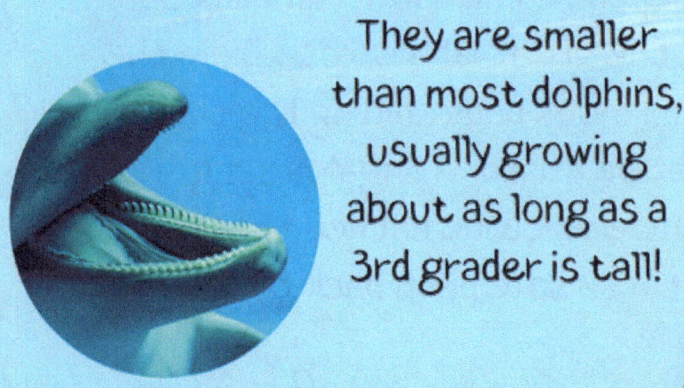

They are smaller than most dolphins, usually growing about as long as a 3rd grader is tall!

They eat fish and squid, which they catch using their sharp teeth and quick moves.

Spinner dolphins have long, thin flippers that help them swim quickly and turn easily in the water.

Their tails, called flukes, are very powerful and help them swim fast and jump high out of the water.

Dolphins stay close to their families, and moms take great care of their babies, called calves.

They live in warm ocean waters all around the world, especially in tropical places like Hawaii.

Spinner dolphins love to be social and live in groups called pods, which can be as small as 10 or as big as 1,000 dolphins!

They use echolocation, like a natural sonar, to find food and see in the dark ocean.

These dolphins "talk" to each other using clicks, whistles, and squeaks. Each dolphin has its own unique whistle.

Spinner dolphins jump out of the water for fun and to show off. Their spins may also help get rid of pesky fish or clean their skin.

Spinner dolphins work together to herd fish into a group, making it easier for each dolphin to grab a tasty bite.

They love to play, chasing each other, racing, and even surfing in waves!

Giant Clam

The giant clam is the largest clam in the world and can grow as big as a suitcase!

Giant clams start life as tiny babies, about the size of a grain of sand, floating in the ocean!

These clams are super heavy and can weigh to 500 pounds (230 kg)!

Giant clams have a special relationship with tiny algae inside them, which use sunlight to make food that the clam can eat.

Giant clams can sense light and dark. They open their shells in the sunlight and close them when something passes over.

Even though they have huge shells, giant clams don't snap shut suddenly. They close their shells slowly.

Giant clams have bright, colorful "mantles" (the soft part inside their shell) in shades of blue, green, purple, and yellow!

The tiny algae inside the clam's body give it energy and help make its bright colors.

Whale Shark

Whale sharks are the biggest fish in the ocean, growing as long as a school bus!

Whale sharks are slow swimmers, usually moving at about 3 miles (4,5 km) per hour.

Even though they're huge, whale sharks are gentle and don't harm people. They mostly eat tiny sea creatures.

Whale sharks often swim close to the surface, making it easy for people to spot them and swim alongside them!

Whale sharks have big, powerful tails that help them move through the water, but they still prefer to cruise slowly.

Their skin is super thick, helping protect them from predators like sharks or even accidental boat bumps.

Smaller fish, called remoras, often stick to whale sharks to get a free ride and eat leftover food from the shark.

Whale sharks love warm, tropical waters where food like plankton is plentiful.

Whale sharks can live for a very long time—some may live up to 100 years!

Each whale shark has unique spots and stripes on its back, like a fingerprint, which helps scientists tell them apart.

They can filter up to 600,000 liters (158,000 gallons) of water in just one hour while searching for food.

Whale sharks are filter feeders, which means they swim with their mouths open to catch food from the water.

They have huge mouths that can open up to 5 feet (1,5 m) wide —but they only eat tiny things like plankton, fish eggs, and small fish.

The Shark God Who Saved Sailors

Kamohoaliʻi, the shark god, loved the people of Hawaii and protected them when they traveled across the ocean.
He often appeared as a large shark with glowing fins, guiding canoes safely through the waves.

One day, a fisherman named Nalu set out alone, hoping to catch enough fish to feed his family. But a fierce storm rolled in, and Nalu's canoe was tossed by huge waves. He lost his paddle and drifted far from land.

As Nalu began to lose hope, he saw a shining fin in the water. A large shark swam beside him. At first, Nalu was afraid, but then he remembered the stories of Kamohoali'i. "Please help me!" Nalu cried.

The shark swam in front of the canoe, leading it through the rough seas. When the storm cleared, Nalu saw the shore in the distance. He paddled with his hands until he reached the beach, safe and sound.

From that day, Nalu always left the first fish he caught in the ocean as an offering to Kamohoali'i, the kind shark god.

Great Hammerhead Shark

Great hammerhead sharks have a wide, flat head shaped like a hammer. That's how they got their name!

Even though they're big, great hammerheads are usually shy around humans and swim away if people get too close.

Great hammerheads are the biggest kind of hammerhead shark. They can grow up to 20 feet (6 m) long—almost as long as a car!

Their skin feels like sandpaper, which helps them glide through the water more easily.

Their hammer-shaped head helps them steer better, turn quickly, and spot prey hiding on the seafloor.

They like to swim alone, unlike some other sharks that live and hunt in groups.

Baby hammerhead sharks are called pups. A mother shark can give birth to 20-40 pups at a time!

Great hammerheads like warm waters and are often found near coral reefs and coastlines in tropical places.

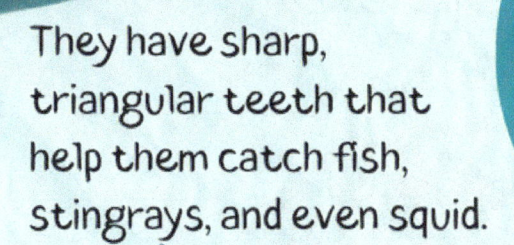

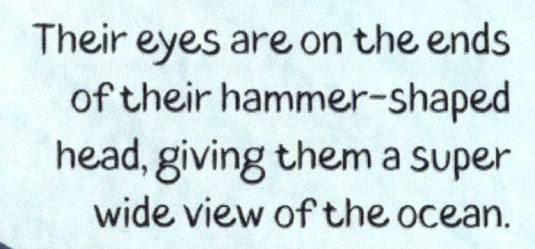

They have sharp, triangular teeth that help them catch fish, stingrays, and even squid.

Their eyes are on the ends of their hammer-shaped head, giving them a super wide view of the ocean.

They love to eat stingrays! Their wide head helps them pin down stingrays before they bite.

Their heads are packed with special sensors that help them "smell" electric signals from other animals nearby!

69

Giant Pacific Octopus

The giant Pacific octopus is the largest octopus in the world.

Giant Pacific octopuses have three hearts! Two pump blood to the gills, and one pumps it to the rest of the body.

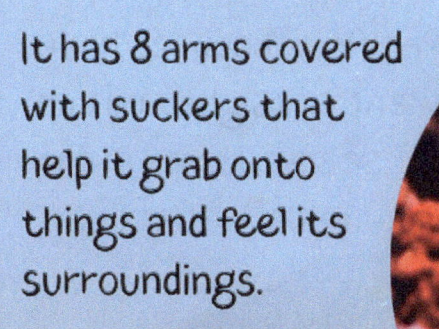

It has 8 arms covered with suckers that help it grab onto things and feel its surroundings.

Each arm has up to 280 suckers, which help the octopus hold onto prey and even taste things!

Their suckers can taste and smell, helping them find food and check if something is safe to eat.

Their blood is blue because it contains copper, which helps them survive in cold ocean waters.

Giant Pacific octopuses have excellent eyesight and can see well even in dim underwater light.

They're one of the smartest sea creatures and can solve puzzles, open jars, and find hidden food.

The octopus can change its color and texture to blend in with rocks, sand, or seaweed to hide from predators.

Their bodies are soft and flexible, so they can squeeze through tiny spaces as small as a quarter!

When they feel threatened, they squirt dark ink to confuse predators and make a quick escape.

A female octopus can lay up to 100,000 eggs! She carefully guards and cleans them until they hatch.

The Octopus
Who Held the World Together

When the world was young and the islands of Polynesia were just being formed, Tangaroa, the god of the sea, chose his most clever creature—the octopus—to help.

The octopus used its eight powerful arms to lift boulders from the ocean floor and place them carefully to form islands for people to live on. But one day, the waves grew wild, and the rocks began to scatter.

The octopus wrapped its arms around the islands, holding them steady until Tangaroa calmed the seas.

"You are the glue that keeps the islands together," Tangaroa said.

To this day, Polynesians honor the octopus as a wise and powerful creature, a reminder of the sea's strength and mystery.

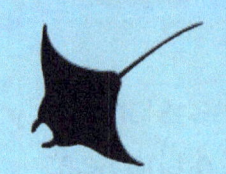

Manta Ray

Manta rays are some of the largest rays in the ocean, with wingspans that can grow as wide as 29 feet

They have two small fins near their mouths that look like horns, which is why they're sometimes called "devilfish"—but they're completely harmless!

Even though they are huge, manta rays are gentle and only eat tiny plankton and small fish.

Manta rays can leap high out of the water, sometimes spinning and flipping in mid-air like underwater gymnasts!

Each manta ray has unique spots and markings on its belly, like a fingerprint, so scientists can tell them apart.

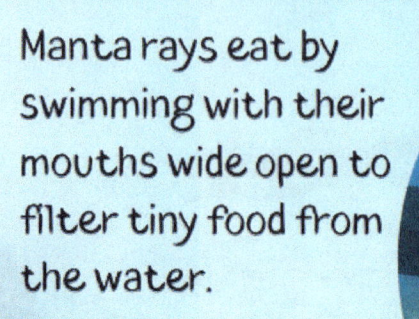

Manta rays eat by swimming with their mouths wide open to filter tiny food from the water.

Manta rays don't chew their food; they just swallow it whole!

They glide through the water so smoothly that they make almost no noise—like silent underwater airplanes!

Like other rays, mantas breathe through small openings called spiracles on the bottom of their bodies.

Manta rays like warm tropical and subtropical waters, so you can find them near Polynesian islands.

Manta rays are excellent travelers and can swim hundreds of miles across the ocean in search of food.

The Manta Ray's Moonlight Dance

In Hawaiian waters, manta rays are known as graceful spirits of the sea. One story tells of Hāhālua, a manta ray who loved the moonlight.

Every full moon, Hāhālua leaped from the ocean, twirling and gliding in the air to honor the moon. The villagers watched in awe, calling it the "Dance of the Rays."

Even today, when manta rays glide through the water, Hawaiians believe they carry the moon's magic, reminding everyone to respect the ocean.

Moray Eels

Moray eels look like long, slimy snakes, but they're actually fish!

Moray eels are a special kind of eel with long, slippery bodies.

They're nocturnal, which means they hunt at night when many other animals are asleep.

They live in coral reefs, rocky areas, and even sandy bottoms of the ocean, helping keep the reef healthy.

Moray eels come in all sizes, from small ones about 1 foot (30 cm) long to giant ones that can grow over 10 feet (3 m)!

They move by wiggling their bodies like a snake to glide through the water.

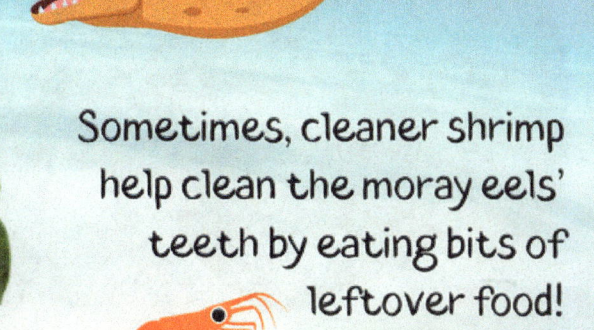

Sometimes, cleaner shrimp help clean the moray eels' teeth by eating bits of leftover food!

Unlike most fish, moray eels don't have scales. Their smooth skin is covered in slippery mucus for protection.

Moray eels like to live alone and don't hang out with other eels very often.

Moray eels come in many colors, like green, yellow, brown, and spotted patterns to blend in with coral and rocks.

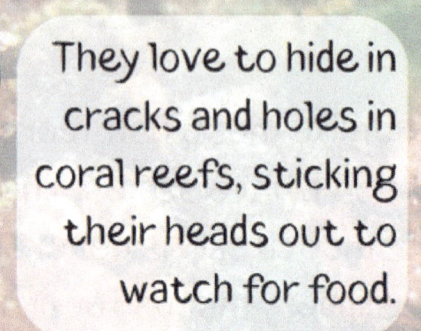

They love to hide in cracks and holes in coral reefs, sticking their heads out to watch for food.

They stay hidden and wait for fish to swim by, then strike quickly to catch their dinner.

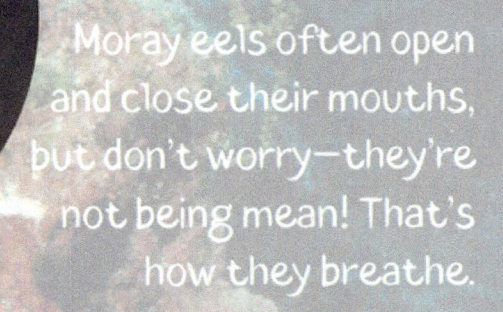

Moray eels often open and close their mouths, but don't worry—they're not being mean! That's how they breathe.

They have a second set of jaws inside their throat, called pharyngeal jaws, to pull food into their mouths!

Moray eels have lots of sharp, pointed teeth that help them catch slippery fish and squid.

Sina and the Coconut Tree

Sina was a young girl who lived in a small Samoan village. She had a pet eel that swam in a sparkling lagoon. She loved the eel and cared for it every day.

But the eel grew larger and larger, and soon Sina realized it was no ordinary eel—it was the spirit of a chief who had fallen in love with her.

One day, the eel spoke to Sina. "When I die, plant my head in the ground, and something wonderful will grow."

Sina felt sad to say goodbye, but she did as the eel asked. From the spot where she buried the eel's head, the very first coconut tree grew.
Its round coconuts had three marks that looked just like the eel's face.

To this day, Samoans tell this story whenever they drink from a coconut. They say it's a gift from the eel spirit, reminding everyone of love, kindness, and transformation.

Clownfish

Clownfish are famous for their bright orange color with white stripes outlined in black.

Clownfish became super famous because of the movie "Finding Nemo"!

Even though they're small, clownfish are strong swimmers and dart quickly around their anemone.

They are small fish, usually only 2 to 5 inches (5 - 12.5 cm) long—about the size of your hand!

Clownfish live in sea anemones, which are their safe homes in the ocean.

Sea anemones have stinging tentacles, but clownfish are immune to them thanks to their special slime coat.

Clownfish help sea anemones by cleaning them and scaring away predators, and in return, the anemones protect the clownfish.

Female clownfish lay eggs on rocks near their anemone home, and the male guards them until they hatch.

Clownfish live in groups, with one big female, a smaller male, and lots of little clownfish.

The biggest clownfish in the group is always the female, and she's the boss of the group!

Not all clownfish are orange; some are yellow, red, or even black with white stripes.

They live in warm waters of the Indian and Pacific Oceans, including coral reefs near Polynesia.

Humuhumunukunukuapua'a
Reef Triggerfish

The name "Humuhumunukunukuapua'a" is the Hawaiian state fish, and it means "triggerfish with a snout like a pig."

Their lips are often bright blue, which adds to their colorful and unique look.

Aloha

Hawaiians love the humuhumu fish and often feature it in songs, stories, and art.

In 1985, the Humuhumunukunukuapua'a was named the official state fish of Hawaii because it's so special and unique!

It can make grunting sounds like a pig, especially when it feels scared or trapped.

They live in coral reefs in warm tropical waters around Hawaii and the Pacific Ocean.

The "trigger" in their name comes from a special spine on their back. They can lock it into place to wedge themselves safely into rocks.

Jellyfish

Even though they're called jellyfish, they're not fish—they're ocean animals called invertebrates because they don't have bones.

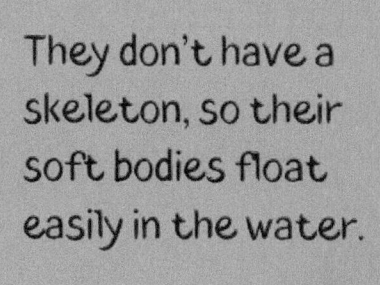

They don't have a skeleton, so their soft bodies float easily in the water.

Jellyfish come in many colors, including pink, blue, purple, and even clear like glass.

Their bodies look like umbrellas or bells, and their tentacles hang down like strings.

Jellyfish are mostly made of water and jelly-like tissue, which makes them squishy and see-through.

Jellyfish don't have a brain, heart, or lungs, but they can still swim, eat, and sense the world around them.

Jellyfish can multiply quickly, sometimes forming massive groups called "blooms" with thousands of jellies!

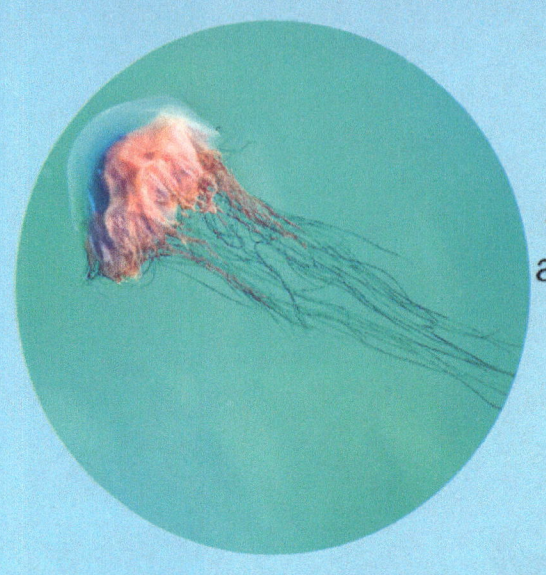

Their tentacles can be super long—sometimes as long as a school bus! They use them to catch food.

Jellyfish tentacles have tiny stinging cells to protect them and catch small fish or plankton.

Most jellyfish stings don't hurt humans, but a few, like the box jellyfish, have powerful stings to be careful of.

DANGER

Some jellyfish glow in the dark! This is called bioluminescence, and it helps scare predators or attract food.

Jellyfish have been around for over 500 million years—long before dinosaurs!

Jellyfish can swim a little, but they mostly drift with the ocean currents.

Some jellyfish are tiny, the size of a pea, while others, like the lion's mane jellyfish, can grow as big as a car!

Roosters and Hens

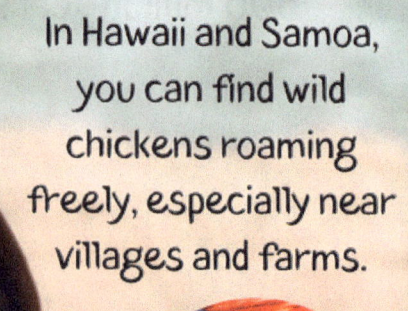

In Hawaii and Samoa, you can find wild chickens roaming freely, especially near villages and farms.

Roosters love to crow in the morning! Their loud "cock-a-doodle-doo" wakes everyone up.

Roosters have colorful feathers on their tails and necks, often shimmering green, blue, or gold.

Hens like to sleep in safe places, like coops or trees, to avoid predators.

In Hawaii and Samoa, chickens have gone wild and live like jungle birds, finding food and shelter on their own.

Hens are the females, and they lay eggs almost every day if they're happy and healthy.

When eggs hatch, baby chicks are covered in fluffy down feathers and follow their mom everywhere!

Chicken eggs can be white, brown, or even blue and green, depending on the breed.

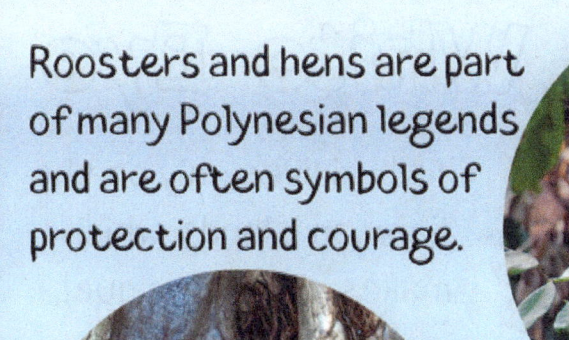

Roosters and hens are part of many Polynesian legends and are often symbols of protection and courage.

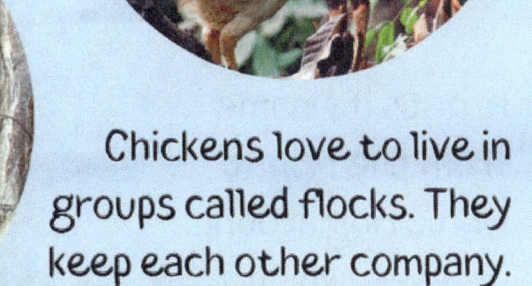

Chickens love to live in groups called flocks. They keep each other company.

Hens like to make soft nests with leaves and grass to keep their eggs safe.

Samoan White-Eye

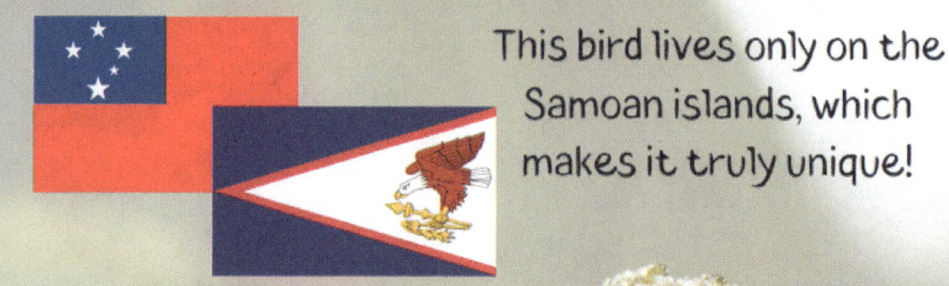

This bird lives only on the Samoan islands, which makes it truly unique!

It gets its name from the bright white ring around its eyes, which looks like it's wearing glasses.

The Samoan White-Eye eats small insects. It also loves to eat berries and small fruits.

Because it's small and green, the Samoan White-Eye can be tricky to find in the trees.

The Samoan White-Eye makes high-pitched chirping sounds to talk to other birds.

The Samoan White-Eye is a tiny bird, only about the size of a ping-pong ball!

These birds love to live in small groups, called flocks, and help each other find food.

The White-Eye is a shy bird that hides high in the treetops.

It builds small, cozy nests out of grass and twigs to lay its eggs.

It's quick and zips through the trees in search of food.

ʻIʻiwi
Hawaiian Honeycreeper

The ʻIʻiwi lives only in Hawaii and can't be found anywhere else in the world.

ʻIʻiwi birds make a variety of whistles, chirps, and squawking sounds to communicate.

The ʻIʻiwi is considered a special bird in Hawaiian culture and appears in many legends.

The 'I'iwi has bright red feathers that make it one of the most colorful birds in Hawaii.

'I'iwi birds love Hawaiian flowers like 'ōhi'a lehua and lobelia for their sweet nectar.

Their tongues are long and tubular, like a straw, to help them sip nectar.

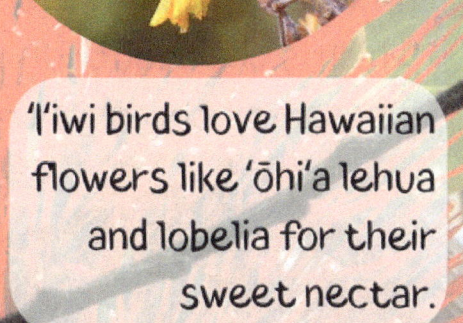

Its long, curved beak is perfect for reaching deep into flowers to sip nectar.

They drink nectar, just like hummingbirds, but they also eat insects and spiders.

ʻŌhiʻa Lehua

The ʻōhiʻa lehua is a special tree that grows only in Hawaii.

The word "lehua" in Hawaiian means "flower," which is the beautiful blossom on the ʻōhiʻa tree.

Its flowers are fluffy and bright red, but they can also be yellow, orange, or pink.

The tree is linked to Pele, the Hawaiian goddess of volcanoes. She's said to protect the ʻōhiʻa.

The fluffy lehua flowers are full of sweet nectar that birds like the ʻiʻiwi love to drink.

This tree is tough! It can grow on hard, rocky lava flows where few other plants survive.

A disease called "Rapid 'Ōhi'a Death" is harming these trees, so people are working hard to protect them.

The 'ōhi'a tree can survive strong winds, heavy rain, and even drought.

Nēnē Hawaiian Goose

You can see Nēnē on the islands of Maui, Hawaii (Big Island), Kauai, and Molokai.

The Nēnē is Hawaii's state bird and only lives on the Hawaiian Islands.

Nēnē have calm, gentle personalities and aren't as loud or aggressive as other geese

It's called "Nēnē" because of the soft, honking sounds it makes, which sound like "nay-nay."

Nēnē have a softer voice than other geese, and their honks are more like gentle whispers.

The Nēnē has been in Hawaii for thousands of years and is very special to Hawaiian culture.

Nēnē Crossing

Their brown, black, and white feathers help them blend in with the Hawaiian grasslands and lava fields.

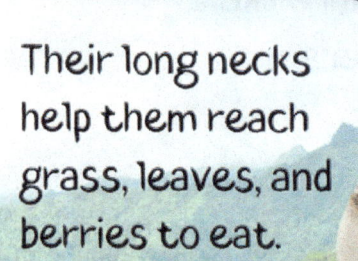

Their long necks help them reach grass, leaves, and berries to eat.

Unlike most geese, Nēnē spend most of their time on land instead of water.

They aren't super-fast runners, but their strong legs help them walk long distances.

Nēnē have special feet with less webbing, making it easy for them to walk on sharp lava rocks.

Nēnē can fly, but they don't migrate like other geese. They stay in Hawaii all year long.

They live in grassy fields, scrublands, and even rocky lava flows where few other animals can survive.

Nēnē live in small family groups and stay close to their flock.

Baby Nēnē, called goslings, are fluffy and gray when they hatch!

Thank you for joining this adventure through the amazing world of Polynesia's animals!

But this isn't the end
—there's still so much to discover!
Keep asking questions, exploring nature, and caring for the amazing creatures we share this world with.

If this book brought you joy, I'd love to hear your thoughts—
leave a review on Amazon to share your experience.
See you in our next wild journey with nature!

Zofia Kos

MORE BOOKS BY THE AUTHOR

YOU CAN FIND IT EXCLUSIVELY ON AMAZON

Made in United States
Orlando, FL
04 March 2025